Einstein

Nigel Hunter

Illustrations by Richard Hook

Bookwright Press
New York · 1987

Great Lives

William Shakespeare
Queen Elizabeth II
Anne Frank
Martin Luther King, Jr.
Helen Keller
Ferdinand Magellan
Mother Teresa
Louis Braille
John Lennon

John F. Kennedy
Florence Nightingale
Elvis Presley
Gandhi
Captain Cook
Napoleon
Einstein
Marie Curie

First published in the
United States in 1987 by
The Bookwright Press
387 Park Avenue South
New York, NY 10016

First published in 1986 by
Wayland (Publishers) Limited
61 Western Road, Hove
East Sussex BN3 IJD, England

© Copyright 1986 Wayland (Publishers) Limited

ISBN 0-531-18092-1
Library of Congress Catalog Card Number: 86-50823

Phototypeset by The Bath Press, Avon
Printed in Italy by G. Canale & C.S.p.A., Turin

Contents

Professor Einstein

Albert Einstein, the greatest scientist of the century, had a theory about socks. They were a waste of time, he said; and he never wore any. Not bothering with socks gave Einstein more time to think about more important things. How did the universe fit together? What was the explanation of it all? Everywhere he went, Einstein kept a pen and notebook handy, in case he had to scribble down some new idea, or make a few quick calculations.

In some ways, he was the picture of the absent-minded professor. There are stories of Einstein returning home from his wedding without his front door key; and, later in life, of phoning the university after going out for a walk, to ask for his own address. At various times he was German, Swiss and American. He was also Jewish, and toward the end of his life was offered the Presidency of Israel. But speaking out for peace among nations, he seemed to many people simply a citizen of the world.

Einstein the international traveler often looked rather comical. With his well-worn overcoat flapping in the breeze, his crumpled trousers, his unruly mop of hair, his pipe in one hand and his violin case in the other, he could almost have been a character acted by Charlie Chaplin. In fact they once rode together in a car in Hollywood. Chaplin pointed to the excited crowd around them, saying, "The people are applauding you because none of them understands you, and applauding me because everybody understands me." Einstein's fame was based on his scientific theories – but many people found them completely baffling. What they did know, however, was that he had opened up a whole new universe of unsuspected wonders.

Einstein's scientific theories made him world famous and people flocked to see him.

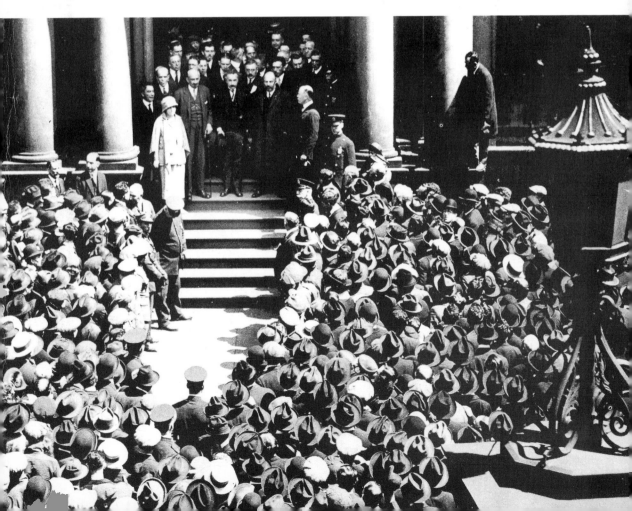

Early stirrings

Einstein was born in the small town of Ulm, in southern Germany, on March 14, 1879. Before his first birthday the family moved to Munich, the provincial capital. Here, his father and uncle owned a small electro-chemical business. His family was Jewish, but they observed none of the religious customs. According to his father, Hermann Einstein, things such as going to the synagogue or not

Albert and his sister Maja were very close in childhood.

Young Albert's mother feared that he was rather a slow learner.

eating ham were just ancient superstitions.

Einstein's mother, Pauline, loved books and music. She encouraged her son to learn the violin, which later became a source of great pleasure to him. He and his younger sister, Maja, enjoyed numerous family outings to the surrounding countryside, with its beautiful lakes and mountains. Perhaps he remembered those days as, years later, he skimmed in his sailboat across the surface of other lakes, amid other hills, in other countries.

As a boy, Einstein seemed slow to learn. He was nine years old before he could speak fluently, and some of his teachers even considered him backward. But deep inside, his sense of wonder and curiosity had been stirring. At the age of five, while he was sick in bed, his father had shown him a compass. The invisible force that kept the needle pointing north intrigued him. So too did his Uncle Jakob's description of algebra, a form of math in which letters stand for numbers. It was a "merry science," his uncle said: "We go hunting for a little animal whose name we don't know, so we call it 'x'. When we bag our game we pounce on it and give it its right name." In his pursuit of scientific truths in later years, math of this kind would be Einstein's main ally.

Albert wanted to understand the force that pointed the compass needle.

Doubts and beliefs

Einstein attended the Luitpold Gymnasium from the age of ten, where he became something of a skeptic and a rebel. He began to question accepted opinions, and the ways in which they were taught. He disliked the school's strict, almost military type of discipline, and later identified it with the spirit of German nationalism that led to two world wars. Only his history teacher encouraged his independent outlook. Many years later, when Einstein was an eminent professor, he called on this teacher. However, he seemed to his old master to be only a

The cathedral of Milan in the city where Einstein joined his family.

Einstein (seated far left) with his schoolfriends at Aarau, Switzerland, 1896.

beggar in shabby clothes, and the visit promptly ended. It seems that he left little impression of his developing talents at school.

Einstein's best work was done at home. It followed a period of intense fascination with religion. Under the influence of the region's strong Catholic faith, he studied the Bible in search of truth. But at the same time – about the age of twelve – he began reading books about science and math. These books were lent to him by a student who visited his family every week. Before long, he became convinced that this was where truth really lay. He quickly overtook his student friend in math, and the two went on to have many deep conversations about science, and the ideas of thinkers throughout the ages. Scientific and mathematical knowledge seemed much firmer ground to Einstein, than the explanations offered by religion. Yet throughout his life, he still sometimes referred to God. For Einstein, God became none other than the principle of harmony and order displayed in the universe at large.

When he was fifteen his family moved to Milan, in Italy, leaving him in Germany to finish his school studies. But within six months he was expelled for being a disruptive influence in class. Gladly turning his back on Germany, Einstein crossed the Alps to Milan.

The student who dined with the family was made very welcome by young Einstein, to whom he lent science books.

Questions and answers

His stay in Italy, though short, was long enough to impress on him a sense of freedom and culture which he found lacking in Germany. He then went to Switzerland. The Federal Institute of Technology (F.I.T.) in Zurich would take any student who could pass the entrance exam – even someone like Einstein, who had no school certificate. At sixteen, he would have been its youngest student; but he failed the entrance exam. However, he had shown exceptional ability in math. For the next year he studied at a school near Zurich.

Life in Switzerland suited Einstein well. He carried out his school work in an atmosphere of energetic and cooperative inquiry. The country was politically tolerant, and internationally neutral; the beauties of its mountainous landscapes were breathtaking. Officially, Einstein was no longer a German. After repeated requests, and quite exceptionally for his age, he had been allowed to renounce his nationality.

Einstein enjoyed the lively atmosphere and political tolerance he found in Zurich.

At seventeen, he passed the F.I.T. entrance exam and started studying for a teacher's degree. He enjoyed many musical evenings and weekend outings to the lakes with his student friends. Here he first discovered the pleasures of sailing alone in a small boat. During lulls in the breeze he would take out his notebook and jot down his latest ideas. His main preoccupation now was physics. After 200 years of general agreement about the nature of the physical universe, scientists were facing a range of new, disturbing questions. Some, including Einstein's teachers, preferred to ignore them; but Einstein intended to look for answers.

He graduated in 1900, and the following year he was granted Swiss citizenship. Finding a permanent job proved very difficult. Meanwhile, he continued his private research into the problems of physics. Most scientists experimented in laboratories. Einstein, with pen and paper, tried to make sense of their results.

Throughout his life, Einstein enjoyed sailing.

The patent office clerk

In 1902 Einstein became a low-grade clerk at the Swiss Patent Office, in Berne. His job was to examine all sorts of models and technical plans sent in by hopeful inventors. He had to see how they worked, and then describe them in writing, fully and precisely, to establish the inventor's legal ownership of the idea. This job had nothing to do with the questions that most concerned him in physics. But in some ways, it was ideal. Puzzles and gadgets had always fascinated him; and his job left him enough time and energy to continue his own line of research. Perhaps it also sharpened his ability to penetrate right to the heart of other people's ideas – to follow their reasoning, and detect any flaws. During spare moments at the office and during the evenings and weekends he worked on the basic problems confronting physicists.

Although he was beginning to publish his ideas in specialist journals, Einstein was still almost unknown among other scientists. But a small circle of

Einstein worked as a badly paid clerk at the Swiss Patent Office.

close friends and admirers was starting to grow around him. Originally, Einstein had offered private lessons in math and physics, to boost his moderate income. But he and his students soon became simply good companions. As a group they gave themselves the high sounding name of the "Olympia Academy." Their shared enthusiasm for science and philosophical discussions, music and walks in the open countryside, greatly enhanced Einstein's social life.

In 1903 he was married. His bride was a friend of his student days, a mathematician named Mileva Maric. Unfortunately, he was later to admit that the marriage was a mistake – that he and his wife were basically unsuited to each other. But professionally, Einstein was on the verge of the century's most astounding scientific breakthrough.

Einstein married Mileva Maric, a mathematician, in 1903.

The "Olympia Academy"—Maurice Solovine, Conrad Habicht, Albert Einstein.

Breaking through

The conclusions Einstein came to in 1905 appeared in five separate papers in a scientific journal called the *Annals of Physics*. The first was good enough to earn him a further degree from the University of Zurich. The others led science into a new age.

Einstein has been called an artist of science. Some experts say that his theories have the same kind of beauty and imaginative vision that you might expect in poetry or art. He strove for the utmost simplicity and clarity. But his papers were written mainly in the language of higher mathematics, which made them incomprehensible to most people. They dealt with spheres of activity which only the specialists fully understood. Each one examined an area of physics beset by contradictions. On the basis of known facts, Einstein first made an imaginative guess, and then worked out the consequences of his idea. He constructed a

Einstein would spend weeks in a state of confusion, pondering over his theories.

richer, deeper, more complete understanding of things.

He established that molecules existed, showing how they could be counted, and how their movement affected temperature. He showed that the energy of light was contained in small packages, now called photons.

With his famous *Special Theory of Relativity* he tackled motion, and the speed of light. It altered the scientific understanding of time, showing how time passes at different rates for observers in different places, depending on their relative movement. Einstein found that speed affects not only time, but a body's mass and length as well. Things in everyday life move too slowly, relative to us, for these effects to be noticeable. But inside the smallest "building blocks" of matter called atoms, events take place at the highest possible speeds. This is where his theory applied. In a mathematical equation that later changed the world, he stated the equivalence of mass and energy: $E = mc^2$.

Einstein giving a talk at the University of Zurich.

Moving on

Einstein was promoted at his office. He remained a clerk in the Patents Department for another four years. But his name was becoming well known among leading scientists.

A mathematician named Hermann Minkowski developed a new form of geometry to measure events in the universe of "Relativity." It combined space and time into one whole: "From now on," Minkowski said, "space by itself and time by itself must sink into the shadows." The experiments that scientists conducted seemed to confirm Einstein's theories.

In 1908 Einstein began teaching part-time, at the University of Berne. The following year, at the age of thirty, he became a full-time

Einstein and Mileva had two sons, Hans Albert and Eduard.

In 1911 the Einstein family moved to Prague, where Einstein becomes a professor.

teacher at Zurich University. Then in 1911, with his wife Mileva and two sons, Hans Albert and Eduard, Einstein moved to Prague. Prague was the Austro-Hungarian capital of Bohemia (in present-day Czechoslovakia). Here he became a full professor. This meant that he and his family could now enjoy a good standard of living. More important to Einstein was the University's magnificent library. Now he worked to extend his special theory and was in regular contact with all the leading scientists of Europe.

Many universities wanted him on their staff. In 1912 he accepted a high appointment at the F.I.T. in Zurich where, as a boy of sixteen, he had failed the entrance exam. Then, in the spring of 1914, Einstein was tempted to Berlin, the capital of Germany. It was said that eight of the twelve people in the world who fully understood his theories lived in Berlin. For his work, conditions seemed ideal. He would be Research Director of the new Kaiser Wilhelm Institute for Physics. But it was an unfortunate time to return to the land of his birth. The world was about to plunge into war.

17

The twisted universe

World War I began in August 1914. Most people considered it a glorious and necessary thing. To Einstein, it was simply mass slaughter. Like the soldiers in the trenches, he was horrified by the new weapons that scientists invented, such as poisonous gas. This was a misuse of science, he believed. Einstein held Germany responsible for the war and helped to write a manifesto for peace and international cooperation. Then he joined a political party that sought an end to the war. This party was outlawed by the government in 1916.

That year, Einstein published his *General Theory of Relativity*. It was the result of ten years' work on the nature of gravity, and how gravity fitted into the space-time universe. This theory has been called the greatest single achievement of human thought. It applied to the stars and distant galaxies, showing how space-time had to be thought of as curved. One way of testing it was to see if gravity affected the beam of light from a star. A British astronomer named Arthur Eddington realized that

Einstein considered poisonous gas used during World War I, to be a misuse of science.

an eclipse of the sun, which was due in 1919, would make the observations possible, and plans for British expeditions to Africa and South America were made. Meanwhile, in 1917, Einstein published yet more work, showing that the universe had no boundary, but neither did it go on forever: it twisted back upon itself; and at that time, his work suggested it was about 1,000 quintrillion km across.

Einstein's Swiss passport meant he could travel, despite the war. He visited scientific colleagues in Holland and

Switzerland, and made contact with people working for peace. He also visited his wife and sons, who had been living in Zurich since the war started. But his marriage was almost over. His public life, however, was just beginning.

Einstein met with astronomers to discuss his theory of the universe.

Out of the shadows

Following his divorce from Mileva, Einstein married his cousin, Elsa Lowenthal.

The post-war years brought many changes in Einstein's life. Following Germany's defeat, which he welcomed, a democratic republican government came to power. His support for this government would lead him to take up German nationality again. A divorce from Mileva was followed by marriage to his cousin, a widow named Elsa Lowenthal. Now he had two grown-up stepdaughters. Also,

for the first time, his Jewish family roots became important to him. Since living in Prague, before the war, he had been aware of the hostility Jews often faced. Now he gave his support to the Zionists, Jews who were working for the creation of a Jewish State in Palestine.

In 1919 came the biggest change of all: Einstein became famous. British expeditions studying the eclipse returned from Principe and Brazil with photographs and calculations that confirmed his *General Theory of Relativity*. "Light caught bending!" read the headlines. Suddenly, the public became aware of how different the universe was from how it seemed. Relativity became the talk of Europe and America. Editors scrambled for writers who could explain it simply. One offered a prize for an article of 3,000 words – jokingly, Einstein said the competition was too hard even for him to enter!

In Germany, he became the target of anti-Jewish prejudice. Certain scientists there called the new theories Jewish physics, and tried to discredit them. But their arguments were feeble: Einstein attended one of their public meetings and showed great amusement at their errors and distortions. However, the situation was serious. During Einstein's first tour abroad, in 1921, a young Berliner was convicted of offering a reward for his murder. As both a pacifist and a prominent Jew, he was to live with the threat of assassination for some time.

At a public meeting Einstein heard a German anti-Jewish speaker distorting the theory of relativity.

Links

In the spring and early summer of 1921, Einstein visited the United States and Britain. He toured the United States, fund-raising for the Zionist cause, and giving university lectures about his theories. He was astonished by the public interest in relativity. With a twinkle in his eye, he explained it like this: "It was formerly believed that if all material things disappeared out of the universe, time and space would

Einstein was very interested in the creation of Israel as a Jewish state. He is seen here in later life with Ben Gurion, the first Prime Minister of Israel.

be left. According to the relativity theory, however, time and space disappear together with the things."

Now the war was over, Einstein stressed the need to renew scientific and cultural links across Europe. He was appalled by the sight of the former battlefields in France, a landscape of blasted villages and

The devastation caused by war appalled the pacifist Einstein.

blackened tree stumps. If only the students of the world could see this, he remarked, they would know how ugly war really is. He believed that a non-competitive, non-patriotic form of education was the key to a peaceful world: that, and a world order based on socialism.

Einstein was awarded the Nobel Prize for Physics in 1922. Many people considered it long overdue. Generously, he gave all the prize money to his former wife, Mileva. Then in 1923, returning from a lecture tour of Japan, he visited Palestine (now called Israel). He officially opened the new Hebrew University in Jerusalem, where he spoke enthusiastically to large and excited crowds about the new possibilities Palestine represented for the Jewish people. He also expressed his admiration for the customs and culture of Palestinian Arabs.

At home, Einstein was in great demand as a famous and distinguished dinner guest. He hated the formalities of such occasions, especially the need to find suitable smart clothing. He did his best to please – but privately, he called these affairs "feeding time at the zoo!"

Einstein received an honorary degree from Princeton University, 1921.

The turning tide

1929 brought new honors. Einstein received the Planck medal.

Toward the end of the 1920s, Einstein began to lose his place at the forefront of scientific thought. A number of new discoveries concerning the smallest known particles of atoms seemed to suggest that certain events occurred simply by chance. This was a challenge to all that was previously known about scientific processes, and Einstein found it impossible to accept. "God does not play dice with the world," he insisted. He was to spend the rest of his life trying to prove this. However, other leading physicists eventually accepted the role of chance, and began to predict the outcome of various processes in terms of probability rather than certainty. Einstein's reputation was secure from his previous work. But in the future, scientifically, he was to become an increasingly isolated figure.

His fiftieth birthday, in 1929, brought many honors, and messages of congratulations from around the world. Over the next few years, he made several trips to the United States where he was especially interested in the giant astronomical observatory at Mount Wilson in California. He also visited Britain, where he gave a series of lectures at Oxford University. He met many celebrities and people from all walks of life.

Everywhere, he vigorously continued his campaign for world peace. In publications and public speeches, he called on the world's workers to stop producing arms and ammunition, and to refuse to serve in their nations' armed forces. This, he believed, was one way to ensure no future wars. For many people, his appeals carried great weight. But for others, they seemed ill-considered and over-simplified. And before long, Einstein himself began to reconsider these ideas.

Einstein campaigned for world peace at public meetings.

Target: Einstein

While Einstein was visiting the United States during the first months of 1933, Adolf Hitler's Nazi Party came to power in Germany. Anti-Jewish hysteria rose to a fever pitch. Once again, his scientific theories were attacked as Jewish physics. Along with the writings of many other Jews, pacifists and anti-Nazis, books by Einstein were banned and publicly burned. His home was broken into and many of his possessions were confiscated or destroyed. His portrait was published on the first page of a book of national "enemies," and underneath it was the caption "Not yet hanged." To return to Germany was out of the question. For the second time, Einstein renounced his German citizenship.

Einstein stayed for a few months in a seaside town in Belgium, and then near a village on the coast of Norfolk, in Britain. Here, he was guarded by two young women with shotguns:

Adolf Hitler's Nazi Party banned books written by Einstein.

there was a rumor that the Nazis had a reward (equivalent to about $5,000) on his head. Wryly, he said he hardly knew it was worth so much. In the face of Nazi aggression toward other nations, Einstein abandoned his purely pacifist principles: now he recommended the formation of an international police force, capable of resisting the Nazis by using weapons if necessary.

At the end of 1933, Einstein and his wife Elsa left Europe for good, to settle in the United States. His welcome was shortly made plain, by an invitation to dine with President Roosevelt, and to stay overnight at the White House. At Princeton University, he continued his scientific research. As always, sailing and music provided his main source of relaxation; but he also turned his mind to minor inventions, helping a friend to develop a new type of camera and refrigerator. Soon, however, he would be linked with the most destructive invention in history.

Einstein relaxed by playing the violin with friends.

Hearts and minds

The atomic bomb was not
Einstein's invention. It was the
work of a team of scientists in a
top secret United States research
center during World War II. But
some of the responsibility was
Einstein's. His equation of 1905,
$E = mc^2$, had stated the basic
principle that made the atomic
bomb possible. And in 1939 he
wrote a letter to President
Roosevelt telling him of the
possibility of this new type of
bomb, and warning of the danger
that the Nazis might develop it
first. The Manhattan project to
build atomic weapons was set up
as the United States entered the
war in 1942. Einstein was not
officially involved, but he knew
of its existence.

He knew, too, when the first
bombs were almost ready for use.
By then, the war was almost
over, and he sent another letter
to the President, urging that
they should not be used. But in
August 1945 two atomic bombs
were dropped on Japan. About
100,000 people were killed
instantly, and many more died
from the after-effects.

poised on the verge of destruction by nuclear warfare. "Science has brought forth this danger," he wrote, "but the real problem is in the hearts and minds of men."

Einstein's fame was almost legendary. A schoolgirl wrote to him to find out whether he really existed. Others said they had received helpful letters from him, solving their homework problems. As for his serious scientific research, he continued it almost until the day of his death, April 18, 1955. As he probably suspected, final conclusions proved out of reach. He was only human, after all.

An atom bomb was dropped on Hiroshima in 1945. The destruction and misery it caused horrified Einstein.

For the rest of his life, Einstein called for the abolition of nuclear weapons. "The war is won, but the peace is not," he declared. In broadcasts, speeches, writings and interviews, he called for international co-operation and a world government. He believed it was the only alternative for a world

Important dates

1879   Albert Einstein born in Germany (March 14).

1880   His family moves to Munich.

1884–9   Attends Catholic primary school.

1889–94   Attends Luitpold Gymnasium.

1895–6   Attends Swiss cantonal school. Renounces German nationality.

1896– 1900   Studies for degree as teacher of physics and math, F.I.T., Zurich.

1901   Takes Swiss nationality. Publishes first scientific "paper."

1902   Begins job at the Patent Office, Berne.

1903   Marriage to Mileva Maric.

1905   Publishes four important research papers, including *Special Theory of Relativity*, effectively founding modern physics.

1906–14   His scientific reputation grows: lecturer/professor at Berne, Prague and Zurich; researching gravity.

1914   Professorship in Berlin. Start of World War I.

1916–17   Publishes *General Theory of Relativity*.

1918   End of World War I.

1919   Divorce from Mileva, marries Elsa Lowenthal.

1919   *General Theory of Relativity* confirmed by eclipse observations: world fame follows.

1921   Zionist and other lecture tours to the United States and Britain.

1922   Visits France. Awarded Nobel Prize for Physics.

1923   Visits Japan, Palestine, Spain. Connections with Hebrew University.

1924–30   Continuing peace work: connections with the League of Nations. Begins search for a unified theory.

1930–3   Further visits to the United States and Britain.

1933   Hitler becomes leader of Germany. Einstein finds temporary refuge in Belgium and Britain; then moves permanently to Princeton University in the United States.

1936   Elsa's death.

1939   Start of World War II.

1941   Takes U.S. citizenship.

1945   Atomic destruction of Hiroshima and Nagasaki ends World War II. Retires from Princeton University.

1946–54   Campaigns against nuclear weapons: connections with the Emergency Committee of Atomic Scientists. Turns down offer of the Israeli Presidency, 1952.

1955   Dies (April 18).

Glossary

Atom An arrangement of particles.

Atomic bomb A weapon that releases energy from a core of atoms, creating an immense explosion.

Eclipse An eclipse of the sun takes place when the moon is positioned between the sun and the earth: for a few minutes, in certain parts of the world, the sun's light may be completely blocked.

Energy The power of something to work, by virtue of its position, state, or motion. Heat and light are forms of energy.

Gravity The force of attraction between material objects. A feature of space-time.

Mass A property of matter, similar to weight: but not varying, as weight does, according to gravitational influences.

Matter A combination of molecules; something with substance and weight.

Molecule A combination of atoms; the smallest part of a chemical substance.

Nationalism Devotion to the interests of a particular nation above the interests of all the world's people.

Nuclear Relating to the center or nucleus of an atom; to the energy that holds it together.

Pacifist Someone who denounces violence and warfare.

Philosophical Concerning ideas and thought.

Relativity The relationship between two different ideas or things, such as time and space.

Republican A political system where the head of state is not a king or queen.

Socialism A political system involving ideals of economic and social equality among people.

Synagogue Church, of the Jewish faith.

Zionist Member of the movement for a Jewish homeland in Palestine, which resulted in the state of Israel.

Books to read

Apfel, Necia H. *It's All Relative: Einstein's Theory of Relativity.* New York: Lothrop, Lee & Shepard Books, 1981.

Dank Milton. *Albert Einstein.* New York: Franklin Watts, 1983.

Einstein, Albert. *Albert Einstein.* Mankato, MN: Creative Education, 1985.

Picture Credits

BBC Hulton 14, 19, 20, 26, 29 (top); Swiss National Tourist Office 10; Topham Picture Library 22 (top), 25, 29; Wayland 6 (top and bottom), 8 (bottom); Zefa 8 (top), 13 (top), 17, 22 (bottom); Zionist Archives 5. Cover artwork by Richard Hook.

Index